MW00424124

THE ANSWER BOOK ABOUT
YOU

By Mary Elting and Rose Wyler

With the help of their daughters
Rachel Folsom and Eva-Lee Baird

Illustrated by Rowan Barnes-Murphy

Publishers • GROSSET & DUNLAP • New York
A Division of The Putnam Publishing Group

Contents

Chapter 1
YOUR MARVELOUS NERVES AND SENSES

What Are Nerves For?

Your nerves are like telephone wires, which carry signals from one phone to another. One kind of nerve carries signals from all over your body to your brain. Suppose you are standing around a campfire, roasting marshmallows and singing "Home, home on the range." Nerves in your skin carry messages to your brain, signaling that you are too hot in front and too cold behind. Other nerves signal your brain that you hear music, and words, see bright flames, smell smoke and taste marshmallows. All of these nerves are sensory nerves.

At the same time, motor nerves bring signals back from the brain to various muscles, making them work. As a result, you open your mouth and pop in another marshmallow, turn around to warm your back and start singing, "Where the deer and the buffalo play."

Another set of motor nerves carries messages from your brain to organs inside your body. When you swallow the marshmallow, stomach muscles begin to churn. Blood vessels expand and bring more blood to those hard-working muscles. And the liver puts out juices for digestion. All this happens automatically, and you never have to think about it.

How Do Nerves Work?

Your nerves make electric current, just as a battery does! How does the current get turned on? In many ways. Here is one example: If you stick a pin in your finger, currents instantly shoot off along nerve fibers to nerves in your brain.

When the current reaches the end of one nerve cell, it has to jump over a gap to the beginning of another nerve cell. The first nerve puts out tiny bits of a chemical to help the current jump across the gap. And in a split second—ouch!

All nerve signals travel very fast—sometimes almost 250 miles an hour.

What Does a Nerve Look Like?

Some nerves are big enough to see. They look like pieces of cream-colored string made of many fine fibers. Other bundles of nerve fibers can only be seen with a microscope.

About 12 million nerve fibers carry messages that link your brain with the rest of your body. All your nerves together make up the nervous system—the most remarkable communication system in the whole world.

Why Do You Get Nervous When You Take Tests?

Does nervousness have anything to do with your nerves? You bet it does! Maybe you feel restless and excited before you take a test.

This all starts in the part of the brain where you begin thinking about a problem. The anxious thoughts cause signals to race along nerves to cells that spill a powerful chemical called adrenalin into your blood. Moments later the adrenalin is at work, making your heart beat faster. It signals your sweat glands to pour out sweat. And it may affect muscles, which tighten up and make your stomach hurt.

But there's a way to beat nervousness. Close your eyes for a few moments. Take five deep, slow breaths and smile to yourself. Picture yourself floating in a swimming pool on a beautiful day. Think of the funniest joke you ever heard and open your eyes. Now that test won't seem so scary.

Why Does Scratching Stop an Itch?

Everyone knows scratching feels good—and nobody knows why. But scientists *can* explain why you get an itch. If pain nerves

in your skin are stimulated a little, you don't feel pain—you feel itchy. A mosquito bite irritates your pain nerves just enough to cause an itch. So do allergies, poison ivy and some diseases.

Probably the best way to stop a mosquito bite itch is to scratch lightly in a circle all around the bite, but not directly on it.

Why is the skin the only part of you that can feel an itch? That is another mystery. You have pain nerves inside your body, but you never get an itchy stomach or an itchy heart.

How Many Senses Do You Have?

Scientists don't agree on the exact number. Your senses tell you about changes that happen inside or outside your body. The ones that bring in the outside world are sometimes called the five senses: hearing, sight, smell, taste, and touch. (Touch includes light touch, pressure, pain, heat and cold.)

But there are really more than those five senses. Others include hunger, thirst, nausea and the sense of balance.

Can You Sharpen Your Senses?

You can sharpen some of them. Your sense of balance, for example, depends partly on how well you can control your muscles. Practice gives you better control. That's why acrobats practice for hours every day.

People can also train themselves to pay attention to tiny differences in taste and smell. Milk tasters, who work for big milk companies, have such well-trained senses that they can even tell what the cows have been eating! Carrots make milk taste fishy. Wild onions that cows munch in spring give milk an onion flavor. If a cow is milked fifteen minutes after she has merely sniffed a bag of onions, a trained milk taster can detect the onion flavor in the milk.

If a tank of fresh milk has a slightly weird flavor, the taster tells the company not to sell it. There may be nothing harmful in the milk, but the peculiar flavor might annoy people who buy it.

You can sharpen your sense of taste, in just the way milk tasters train themselves. Put ¼ teaspoon of salt and 1 cup of water into a large jar, shake, and take a sip. If you can taste the salt, add another cup of water to the jar and try again. Keep adding water until you can't taste the salt at all. Now wait a day and try the same thing again. With practice you'll be able to detect smaller amounts of salt than you could the first day.

What Makes a Smell a Smell?

"Spearmint!" The girl sitting behind you is chewing gum, and your nose tells you what kind it is.

You don't smell with your whole nose. Your odor-detectors are just a small patch of cells at the very top of each nostril. This patch is about the size of your thumbnail, and each of its cells is tipped with fringes— millions of them. Somehow these fringes pick up clues that tell what you are smelling. How do they do it? Scientists aren't sure, but they think they can explain what happens.

13

Tiny bits—molecules—of spearmint come floating through the air. All of them have a very special shape that only spearmint molecules have. Like keys that fit only into the right locks, spearmint molecules fit only into the right odor-detectors on the cell fringes in your nose. The moment the key is in the lock a message goes out over nerves from the detector cells to your brain. And you say, "Spearmint gum!"

If you never smelled spearmint again for forty years, you would probably still remember it.

There are some things that you can't smell. Oxygen is one. Probably its molecules don't fit any of your locks. But you *can* identify about ten thousand different odors. A single molecule is the clue to some of them. Other smells, such as the aroma of coffee, come from a mixture of molecules.

How Do Taste Buds Work?

Your taste buds are taste detectors. Each one is a small onion-shaped bunch of cells in the crack around a bump on your tongue. You taste sweet things with the buds at the tip of your tongue. That's one reason why you like to lick lollipops and ice cream cones.

Detectors for a salty taste spread along the front edges of your tongue. Sour detectors are a little farther toward the rear. The buds that taste bitter things are in the center at the back.

The taste of a food almost always depends on the cooperation of several different detectors in your mouth and nose. Lemonade is a combination of sweet and sour, and its odor tells you it was made from lemons, not oranges. Peaches taste sweet, sour and slightly bitter, and they have a special fruity smell.

Once in a while you can fool your taste buds. If you eat an artichoke it will make the next food you eat taste sweet.

A baby has taste buds inside the cheeks and on the roof of the mouth, as well as on the tongue. As the baby grows older, all taste buds except those on the tongue gradually disappear.

Why Doesn't a Squeeze Hurt Like a Pinch?

Squeeze a big chunk of your arm between your fingers. You feel pressure but it doesn't actually hurt. Now, with your fingernails, pinch a little of the top skin on the arm. This hurts.

What you feel each time depends on nerve endings in your skin. One kind of nerve ending detects pressure. Another kind detects pain. Most of your pain detectors lie close to the surface of your arm. So a pinch of the top skin fires off a lot of urgent pain messages to the brain. But the nerve endings that detect pressure are buried deeper down in a cushion of flesh. So when you squeeze a big chunk of your arm your brain mainly gets pressure signals.

Another kind of nerve ending in your skin detects gentle pressure. The slightest touch sends a signal to the brain. Blow ever so gently on your arm, and you'll feel your breath on the hairs growing there. Hairs all over your body help you to feel a light touch. Luckily, your brain gets used to light touch signals. If it didn't, your clothes would drive you crazy!

How Do We See?

The front of the eye is somewhat like a camera. It has a lens that collects rays of light. Just as the camera has film, the back of the eye has a special layer that changes when light strikes it. Light bleaches the material in the eye film and makes patterns there.

The living film in the eye is made of many cells. Some of the cells are shaped like rods. An eye has about 100 million of these. Other cells look like sharpened pencils. They are called cones, and an eye has about six million of them. The cones allow us to see color. The rods show everything in black, white and gray.

All of these millions of cells have nerve connections to the brain. When a pattern of light flashes onto the film of rods and cones, millions of electric signals make a pattern inside the brain, and we see.

What Good Are Tears?

The cells on the surface of your eyes can't live if they dry out. Tears keep them wet. If you get a speck of dirt in your eye, a rush of tears will wash it away. Every minute of the day, bacteria float out of the air into your eyes. Tears get rid of them with a special chemical called an enzyme. The enzyme in tears attacks a germ's outside covering. Acting like a pair of scissors, it cuts holes in the fine net that holds a germ together. The enzyme snips and snips till the whole germ falls apart. Tears wash away the remains. This keeps your eyes from getting infections.

Tears are formed in tear glands—small pouches underneath your upper eyelids. Before you were about four weeks old, your tear glands could form only a small amount of tears. So you could holler, but you couldn't really cry.

Why Do You Blink?

Blinking spreads tears over the surface of the eye and keeps it wet. You blink about once every two to ten seconds. Most people can't keep themselves from blinking for as long as a minute, unless they have their eyes open under water. When you add up all the time spent blinking, you probably spend about a half-hour during the day with your eyes closed.

Chapter 2
THE INSIDE STORY

What Are You Made Of?

If you weigh eighty pounds, more than fifty of those pounds are water. The rest is a batch of chemicals. But the water isn't just sloshing around inside you. It's mixed with the chemicals to form cells of many different kinds. Cells are so small that you have to use a microscope to see them, and it takes about fifty trillion of them to make someone your size.

Cells, Tissues, Organs— What Are They?

Every cell in your body is like a little bag with a life of its own. It takes in food and uses it for energy. It gets rid of wastes. It produces new cells just like itself. But none of your cells could live all by itself outside your body. They need one another, because they share the work of keeping each other alive.

There are many different kinds of cell, each shaped so that it can do a particular job. Muscle cells are long and thin and strong. Little round cells store tiny globs of fat. Bone cells are hard. Long, thin nerve cells with spidery ends carry messages from the brain to muscles.

Groups of cells of the same kind make up tissues. Muscle cells form muscle tissue. Nerve cells form nerve tissue.

An organ, such as your heart, is made of different kinds of tissue, grouped together to do a special job. Your stomach is an organ. So is your brain. You have dozens of others —liver, eyes, kidneys, lungs. Even your skin is an organ.

How Big Is Your Heart?

Your heart is a hollow muscle, only about as big as your fist. When you were born, it weighed less than a small plum, and it will weigh less than a pound by the time you are grown. Yet it has remarkable strength. It pumps about two thousand gallons of blood each day. It will beat about 2.5 billion times and pump about fifty million gallons of blood in your lifetime. If your hand had to do all that pumping, just imagine how tired it would get.

What Is Blood Made Of?

By the time you grow up, you will have about six quarts of blood. About three of those quarts are plasma—a liquid which is mostly water, along with a lot of chemicals. Blood cells floating in the plasma make up the other three quarts.

White cells in the blood gobble up germs.

Tiny broken pieces of another kind of blood cell are called platelets. They help to seal up cuts.

Red blood cells contain a chemical called

hemoglobin that makes them red. Hemoglobin picks up oxygen and carries it to the other cells all over the body. Each red blood cell contains about 280 billion molecules of hemoglobin!

Every day your body makes 20 billion new red cells, and 20 billion old ones are removed from the blood and destroyed. Each red blood cell lives about 120 days. In that time, it makes about 172,000 trips through the vessels that carry blood around your whole body.

What Are Hiccups?

A case of hiccups is a case of mixed-up signals to your diaphragm—a big sheet of muscle that separates your chest from your abdomen. Usually the diaphragm moves smoothly up and down all by itself. It goes down to let air into your lungs, up to push your breath out. Special nerve signals control this automatic action, and you never have to give breathing a thought. But once in a while the signals begin coming too close together. Your diaphragm makes quick, jerky bounces

down and up. At the same time, a strange signal goes to muscles in the voice box in your windpipe. The muscles snap together, and that makes the *hic* in hiccup.

Sometimes you can stop hiccups by holding your breath for a while. Drinking from the wrong side of a cup, or eating a teaspoonful of sugar, or an unexpected smack on the back may interrupt the mixed-up signals. And the hiccups stop.

How Much Air Do You Need?

An adult's lungs take in about 3,300 gallons of air every day. That sounds like a lot, but it would fit into a small room eight feet long, eight feet wide and eight feet high.

Maybe you picture your lungs as big hollow bags that fill up with air when you breathe in. They are nothing of the sort. Each lung is packed with 150 million tiny bubble-shaped air sacs—alveoli—that look like bunches of grapes. Every one of the alveoli is surrounded by tiny blood vessels with walls so thin that oxygen from fresh air can pass right through into the blood. If the alveoli could be flattened out, they would cover an area as big as a tennis court.

How Long Can You Hold Your Breath?

Most of the time you don't think about breathing. About every four seconds, a special part of your brain automatically sends signals to the muscles that let air in and out of your lungs. But if you want to, you can decide to hold your breath. The thinking part of your brain then stops the automatic signals. If you take in a lot of air, you can probably wait for thirty seconds before you have to breathe out.

No matter how hard you try, you can't hold your breath very long. As soon as there is a dangerous lack of oxygen in your body, the automatic signals go into action again. You fill your lungs with air, whether you want to or not.

What Happens to a Cracker When You Eat It?

A cracker is made of hundreds of different chemicals. The main one is starch. Bread and potatoes and noodles are mostly starch, too.

A molecule of starch is very small, but still too big to get into your body's cells where it can be used for energy. It must be chopped into much tinier molecules. Your digestive system does the chopping.

As you chew a cracker, chemicals called digestive enzymes in your saliva go to work. They start breaking up starch molecules. Enzymes in the intestine finish the job. When the starch molecules are small enough, they slip into the cells that line the intestine. From there they move on into the blood which carries them to hungry cells.

What Does an Enzyme Do?

If you had eyes more powerful than the best microscope, you would see that each enzyme is a tiny glob with a pocket in one side. The pocket in a certain kind of digestive enzyme is just the right size to hold a certain part of a starch molecule, the way a lock holds a key. With a piece of the starch molecule locked in, the pocket changes shape for a split second. Somehow it snaps the starch molecule in two! This happens again and again, until the starch is completely chopped into very tiny bits.

There are over two dozen different kinds of digestive enzyme, each with its own kind of pocket. Working together, they chop up almost everything you eat.

Enzymes work astonishingly fast. In just one second, a single digestive enzyme can break apart almost 20,000 starch molecules. Other enzymes work even faster. The speediest one can make changes in more than half a million molecules every second!

Can a Cell "Self-Destruct"?

Believe it or not, a cell can sometimes destroy itself.

Almost all cells contain a little bag with destructive chemicals inside. Some scientists call this the "suicide bag." If there is a leak in the bag, the chemicals—digestive enzymes—will spill out and destroy the whole cell.

Suppose a germ gets into a white blood cell. An amazing thing happens. The suicide bag folds itself around the germ, and there, inside the bag, the enzymes digest the intruder. Digestion breaks the germ up into tiny molecules of different chemicals. Sometimes the bag can gobble up and digest twenty germs at once. The bag can also wrap itself around worn-out parts of a cell and digest them. Often the cell can use these digested parts to build new parts that replace worn-out ones.

The suicide bags in your skin cells break if you get a sunburn, because radiation from the sun makes holes in the bags. Then enzymes leak out. They digest their own home cells, and this makes blisters form on your skin.

At times, your body has to get rid of certain parts. As you grow, your bones change, and they won't be shaped right unless parts of them are destroyed. The cells that aren't needed "self-destruct." Their suicide bags break, and enzymes digest the cells. The leftover chemicals are carried away by the blood or taken in and used by nearby cells.

The same thing happens to tadpoles. When a tadpole becomes a frog, it slowly loses its tail. Using the suicide bags, the cells in the tail self-destruct.

What Is a Gland?

A gland is a group of cells that make special chemicals. The gland itself doesn't use them. Instead, it sends them on to other parts of the body where they have jobs to do. Tear glands make tears which travel through little tubes to the eyes. Another kind of gland puts chemicals directly into blood vessels, and the blood carries them to organs that need them.

What Is a Hormone?

You are walking down a dark path in the woods. Suddenly you hear a ferocious roar. In a few seconds, your heart begins to pound. Breathing speeds up, and you run—faster than you have ever run before.

The cause of all this action in your body is a tiny bit of adrenalin—a chemical that your adrenal gland squirts into your blood when you are scared. The blood carries it quickly to various parts of your body and makes them prepare for action. Cells in your heart begin to work harder. Your liver puts extra sugar into your blood to give your muscles energy.

Adrenalin is a hormone, one of a group of powerful chemicals that act like messengers. Each is made in a special gland, then released into the blood to carry its particular message to other parts of the body. Growth hormone makes your bones grow. Insulin lets your cells take sugar from your blood. And sex hormones make sex organs ready, changing a girl into a woman and a boy into a man.

Why Did You Have More Bones at Age Five Than You Have Now?

Probably you have heard that a skeleton has 206 bones. This is not always true. The number of bones in the body keeps changing. You were born with 270 of them. Some were small pieces of bone called bony centers. For a while new bony centers formed, bringing the total to 443. As you grew, many of these joined together, so that you now have fewer bones. By the time you are old enough for a driver's license, you will be left with only 206. Many years from now a few more of your bones will join together. When you are very old you will have fewer than 200 bones in your skeleton.

How Do Muscles Work?

When you do push-ups you may think the muscles in your arms are shoving you off the floor. The fact is, none of the muscles are pushing. They can only pull. Each time a muscle pulls, it contracts—that is, it gets shorter. When you do a push-up, muscles at the back of your arms contract. This pulls your arms out straight. Then, when you want to bend your arms again, those muscles relax while the muscles at the front of your arms contract.

Muscles are made of cells that are long and thin and soft. Yet when a cell contracts, its soft insides become thick and hard. This can happen because the soft stuff is made of separate threads that slip back and forth.

When they slide toward each other, they bunch up, making the cell harder and shorter. A thick, hard cell is strong enough to lift a thousand times its own weight! When the threads slip back, the cell relaxes and gets long and soft again.

Muscles that do heavy work, such as push-ups, are made of red muscle cells. They don't get tired easily. Another kind—white muscle cells—do tire quickly. They are in your hands and eyes and other parts of your body that make fine, precise movements.

Do You Have a Built-in Clock?

Some people can decide to wake up at 6:53 A.M., and, sure enough, they do. Maybe you can't do that, but your body does have a regular daily rhythm. You probably sleep about eight hours a night. Your temperature goes up in daytime and down at night, and the speed of your heartbeat varies.

Scientists have also found that each organ in your body—even each chemical—has its own rhythm. All of these rhythms seem to depend on built-in clocks, and usually they all work together so that you don't even notice them. Sometimes, however, they can

be upset. If you fly a long way in a plane, you may feel unusually tired and grumpy. This is called jet lag, and it means that some of your clocks have been forced out of harmony with the others.

Sickness can also interrupt the way the clocks work. So can certain medicines. In fact, if a medicine is taken at a certain time of the day, it may help you much more than if you took it an hour earlier or an hour later.

Where are your body's clocks? Scientists haven't completely solved that mystery, but they have some clues. They have discovered that even tiny one-celled bacteria have clocks! Perhaps the clocks "tick" when tiny particles charged with electricity pass back and forth through the bacterium's cell wall. Perhaps the clock is disturbed when unusual chemical changes go on inside the cell. Possibly that is how your clocks work, too.

Chapter 3
YOUR OUTSIDES

How Can You Make
a Wart Go Away?

Warts are mysterious. They can start to grow all of a sudden in the top layer of your skin, usually on your hands or feet. They may last for a long time. Or, after just a little while, they may drop off suddenly, and you would never guess they had been there. Scientists know that a kind of germ called a virus causes warts. The virus makes a group of skin cells multiply very quickly. But scientists don't know why warts disappear.

Some people used to think that a certain kind of grasshopper could cure a wart by biting it. Others rubbed their warts with pennies, or with a raw potato or with rainwater from a rotten stump. Often these strange cures really did work.

Doctors have done experiments that cured warts in an astonishing way. They hypnotized patients and told them that the warts on the left side of the body would drop off. Sure enough, the experiment worked—except for one person. He couldn't tell left from right, and the warts on his *right* side vanished. What was going on here? The doctors still don't know.

Some scientists think that antibodies cure warts eventually. Antibodies are chemicals that your body makes to get rid of a virus. Other doctors think there must be a different type of sensible explanation for the cures that seem to work by magic.

Warts aren't dangerous. But it's not a good idea to poke at them or irritate them. If you break the skin they may get infected. If they grow on the bottom of a foot, they can make walking painful. A doctor can remove them by burning them with an electric needle or by freezing them. A pain-killer keeps the operation from hurting.

Does Chocolate Give You Pimples?

Lucky you—if you like chocolate—for the answer is no. Skin specialists used to blame pimples on chocolate and nuts. Now they say that these things do not cause pimples, though there are other foods that may. Artichokes, for example.

The main reason teenagers get pimples is that they are growing up, and their skin is getting oily. The oil comes from tiny pouches called sebaceous glands underneath the skin. A little bit of oil helps keep the skin smooth and soft, but too much oil may plug the opening to the gland. The plug hardens, and oxygen in the air darkens the top of it forming a blackhead.

This hard oily stuff makes great food for germs. They grow and multiply underneath the blackhead and produce a kind of acid. This is a signal for germ fighters—your white blood cells—to go to work. The battle produces a small glob of yellow pus made of dead germs and white blood cells. That is a pimple.

As you grow older, your skin usually becomes less oily. Fewer and fewer pimples form. Meanwhile, a doctor can prescribe medicines that will help.

What Are Calluses Made Of?

Calluses are hard spots on the skin of hands or feet. Bongo drum players have callused fingertips. People who walk barefoot on rocky paths every day can get calluses as thick as shoe soles on the bottoms of their feet.

You can stick a pin in a callus and it won't hurt, because a callus is simply a layer of dead skin. When skin is alive, it is made of tiny, soft, six-sided cells. These grow in a layer just below the outside surface. New skin cells are constantly forming, and as they grow the top ones are pushed outward. They become flat and dry, and they stick together in a very thin sheet. This sheet of outside skin is flexible and almost waterproof, and it keeps germs out. It also keeps your body fluids in.

Millions of skin cells die and are pushed outward every day. Millions at the surface flake off. But they are so tiny you don't often notice that they are peeling. Usually there is a balance between the number that die and the number of new cells that form. But not always. If there is pressure on the soft, living cells, they multiply faster. These new cells are pushed outward before the old dead ones have had time to flake off. If the pressure continues day after day, the sheet of dead cells becomes a thick protective callus. But if you stop walking or working, your calluses slowly wear away.

Why Do Fingernails Grow?

Fingernails grow from roots! You can't see the roots because they lie beneath the skin at the base of each nail. Nail roots are made of soft living cells.

As new root cells form, the older ones fill up with a hard substance and die. These dead cells flatten out, stick together and become the hard, dry plates that we call nails. Meanwhile, the living cells keep multiplying and pushing the dead ones outward. The nail plates get longer.

As nails lengthen, they seem to creep over the bed of flesh underneath them. Actually, a nail is firmly attached to the bed, except at the fingertip. So the cells in the bed must somehow travel along with the nail plate.

A white half-moon often shows at the base of a nail. At this spot the nail is still a little soft. When it has hardened, it will be translucent, and the pink bed will show through.

The nails on your middle fingers grow faster than any others. All of your fingernails grow more quickly if you play the piano, type or do other things that put pressure on your fingertips.

Why Does a Cut Stop Bleeding?

If you cut yourself, you slice into blood vessels, and blood spurts out of the holes. The leak must be stopped fast. Within fifteen seconds the job is almost done.

First, the blood vessels tighten, causing less blood to flow from the wound. Next, tiny pieces of cells called platelets stick to the edges of the cut. They clump together and slow the blood still more. Finally, clots form and plug the holes. Making a clot is a very complicated business. It takes about thirty different chemicals that are always present in the blood. Each chemical changes the next one in line until the last one turns some of the liquid in the blood into a blob of stuff that's like gelatin. Bleeding stops.

A scab is a clot that has dried out and hardened. It is reddish because the gelatin-like stuff catches red blood cells as it jells.

Your hole-closing system is a life saver. Without it you would bleed to death from a tiny scratch.

How Do Scars Form?

Soon after a cut stops bleeding, new blood vessels begin to grow. At the same time, the cells around the wound produce something called connective tissue. This tissue gradually fills the gap and pulls the sides of the cut together.

Scars look different from the rest of your skin. That is because the connective tissue contains no hair, no sweat glands, and no oil glands.

What Gives Your Skin Its Color?

There are several different kinds of cell in the skin. One very special kind produces tiny specks of a dark brown chemical called melanin. Does this mean that people with dark skin have more of these special cells than light-skinned people? The answer is no. The only difference is in the amount of melanin that each of the special cells produces. If they produce just a little of the chemical, the skin will be light-colored or pinkish. If they produce a great deal, the skin will be dark brown—so dark that it looks black.

Most people in the world have a lot of melanin in their skins. There may also be a yellow coloring material called carotene in fat cells beneath the skin. Different combinations of melanin and carotene result in various colors, from light golden to dark brown.

Why Do You Get Sunburned?

Certain rays of sunlight—the ultraviolet rays—pass through the thin outer layer of your skin. When they reach the inner layer, they beat on sensitive, growing skin cells and damage some of them. Too many damaged cells mean painful sunburn.

People with very light-colored skin get sunburned most easily. Darker skin is protected in an amazing way by tiny bits of the chemical melanin. The melanin is produced in spidery-looking cells with long branches that grow in among the regular skin cells. Every once in a while, a regular cell snips off the end of a branch, and a grain of melanin pops into the cell.

Now the melanin moves to the part of the cell closest to the outside of the body. There it acts like an umbrella. It actually stops the ultraviolet rays.

Ultraviolet light has a special effect on the melanin cells. It makes them begin to produce more melanin. This gives a tan color to light-colored skin. The suntanned skin now has extra protection against sunburn.

Even the darkest black people can get sunburned, because melanin does not enter and protect every single cell in the skin.

Why Do Some People Get Freckles?

Children whose parents have freckles usually get them, too. But no one is born with freckles. Babies must be out in the sun before the small brown spots appear.

Freckles are made of melanin, the same brown chemical that gives the skin a suntan. Some people tan evenly, because all their melanin-producing cells make the same amount. If some cells make more melanin than others, then freckles develop.

What Gives Your Hair Its Color?

Every hair on your head has three layers. A thin, soft inside core is surrounded by a harder thicker layer, with a thin coat of tiny scales outside.

Hair color comes from the thick middle layer, which contains millions of tiny grains of melanin, the same chemical that gives skin its color. These grains can be brownish-black, or reddish-gold, or the two may be mixed together. The grains of coloring material may be large or small, close together or far apart. Hair color depends mainly on the mixture.

The scales on the outside of a hair are colorless, and if they lie flat, the hair will

shine and seem lighter. If the scales are rough, the hair will look darker.

As people get older, their hair seems to turn gray. Actually, there is no such thing as gray hair. It is just a mixture of white hairs and hairs of other colors. A white hair does not have any coloring material at all.

What Makes Hair Straight or Curly?

Each hair on your scalp grows out of a tiny tube in the skin. At the bottom of each tube is a bulb that is constantly making hair cells. As new cells form, old ones die and dry up, and the new cells push the dead ones out of the tube. The hair you see is really just a thread of dead cells. That's why it doesn't hurt when you cut it.

If the new cells grow evenly all around, the hair will be straight. But if more cells are added to one side of the hair, that side will be longer. The long side will wrap around the shorter side, giving the hair a spiral shape, like a spring. If one side of the hair grows much faster than the other, the hair will be very curly.

Chapter 4
WHAT YOUR BODY NEEDS
AND DOESN'T NEED

Why Do We Need to Sleep?

A high-school boy once stayed awake for eleven days without sleeping a wink, as part of a scientific experiment. At the end of the eleventh day, he slept for fourteen hours, stayed awake for the next twenty-four, and slept for only eight hours before going back to a normal life.

Very few people could do that. If they are awake for more than two days, they begin to have weird feelings and to behave in unusual ways. Soon they cannot keep their eyes open.

Usually we are tired at the end of the day, and when we say we want to rest, we mean resting both the body and the brain. The strange thing is that the brain does not seem to rest during sleep. Instead, it is constantly at work, dreaming or remembering or sorting out all the things that happened the day before. Scientists know this from experiments that show how active the brain is during sleep. But they do not know exactly *why* people need to sleep.

Who Needs Vitamins?

Everyone does. You need vitamins to stay alive. Your body uses only very tiny amounts of these chemicals. Yet if you don't get enough of them, you won't grow properly or feel healthy. Since your body does not make its own vitamins, you must get them from food.

Scientists have discovered thirteen vitamins—A, C, D, E, K, and eight different B vitamins. No one food contains all of these. To get all of them, you have to eat many kinds of food. Since sugar contains absolutely no vitamins, it's a good idea to eat fruit instead of candy, soda pop and other sugary junk foods. A junky diet with too few vitamins can make you feel grumpy and sick. You won't look your best, either.

Do You Have to Drink Milk and Eat Meat?

Some people can't drink milk, even if they like it! Newborn babies may become allergic to cow's milk. In some parts of the world people lose their ability to digest milk as they grow up.

Animals do not drink milk after they grow up. A few thousand years ago, before people learned to raise cows and goats and sheep, adults didn't drink milk. In countries where farmers have raised cows for a long time, people are usually able to digest cow's milk.

If milk doesn't upset you, it is a wonderful food. It contains protein, vitamins, calcium and other minerals that your body needs. Calcium is the stuff that holds cement blocks together. It also keeps you on your feet, since your bones are mostly calcium. Milk contains more of it than any other food. If you can't drink milk, you can still have strong bones. But you have to be careful to eat other foods that contain calcium.

Many people never eat meat and are perfectly healthy. They, too, have to be careful to eat other nourishing food. Food from plants contains less protein than meat, milk and eggs, but vegetarians can still get all the protein they need. They must eat special combinations of foods, such as beans and rice, and they must avoid junk food.

What Is the Best Kind of Exercise?

"I run five miles a day and I feel terrific!" That's what many joggers say. But it looks hard. How can it make you feel so good?

At first it *is* hard. But if you keep at it your legs get stronger. You can run farther and faster without feeling tired. In fact, you have more energy all day long. Many people even say they are more cheerful. And of course, athletes jog to build up their strength for other sports.

Jogging is good for the heart. So are hiking, bicycling, swimming and any other active sport. When the heart's muscle fibers grow stronger, it can pump more blood with each beat. This means that it can beat more slowly. Since it gets more rest between beats, it may last longer.

The best kind of exercise is the kind you like to do at least three times a week. If you hike or bike, choose a route that keeps you going for an hour or more at a brisk pace. And make sure you move fast enough to huff and puff a little. It's important to give your heart a good workout. That is why active sports are better than exercises that just make your arm or leg muscles stronger. Sports are more fun too, and so you feel like doing them longer and more often.

If you want to start getting into shape, ask your gym teacher what kind of exercise program would be best for you.

Who Gave the First Vaccination?

Eight-year-old James Phipps was not happy. Dr. Edward Jenner had just cut a small slit in James's arm and rubbed it with some yellow stuff.

"Poor Phipps," the doctor said, but he was sure that James would live through the experiment. He did.

At that time, almost two hundred years ago, many people had died of the contagious disease called smallpox. This disease causes sores filled with pus to form on the body.

Dr. Jenner had no idea that germs caused smallpox. But he did know about a similar disease that caused sore spots on cows. The women who milked the cows got the cowpox sores on their hands. These sores didn't harm the women, and after the spots healed the women never had those sores again. More important, the women never caught the human disease, smallpox.

The liquid from a milkmaid's sore is what Dr. Jenner had used on the boy's arm. James, too, got a few sores, but they healed. Dr. Jenner wanted to prove that James would not get smallpox. So six weeks later he took pus from a patient who had smallpox and rubbed that into James's arm. James never got the disease and was protected from it for the rest of his life. So were many other people whom Dr. Jenner treated. Yet no one knew why.

After many years scientists solved the smallpox mystery. They now know that a germ called a virus made the cows sick. There were viruses in the yellow liquid that Dr. Jenner used. Inside James's body the germs multiplied. And at the same time they created enemies for themselves. They excited the boy's own special germ-fighting cells. These cells began to pour out chemicals called antibodies. Soon trillions and trillions of pox antibodies were in James's blood. There they attached themselves to viruses. The antibodies made it impossible for the germs to multiply. Later, white blood cells surrounded and digested the viruses.

The pox germs were gone but not forgotten. Special "memory cells" remained in the boy's body. When the doctor planted more pox viruses in James's arm, the memory cells began producing antibodies so fast that he did not get the disease. The wonderful thing was that cowpox viruses were weak, but

they left memory cells that could fight the stronger smallpox viruses.

Dr. Jenner called his experimental treatment *vaccination*. Today, so many people have been vaccinated that the disease hardly ever occurs.

Why Do Children Have to Get Shots?

Diseases such as measles and whooping cough haven't disappeared, and children have to be protected against them. Unlike James Phipps, they get shots that hardly hurt. With a thin, sharp needle the doctor injects a bit of liquid under the skin. Sometimes doctors use one shot that will immunize a child from three different diseases. Most children now get oral vaccines, instead of shots, to prevent polio.

As you get older, you may need occasional "booster" shots to keep you protected.

A wound from something like a rusty nail can allow a certain kind of germ to enter the body. The germs produce a poison that can cause a painful disease called tetanus. Many doctors recommend that children and some adults be immunized against tetanus regularly.

If you travel to another country, you may have to be inoculated to keep from getting a disease that is common in that country.

Why Do Germs Make You Sick?

There are two main kinds of germ—bacteria and viruses. Bacteria are tiny one-celled things that live everywhere—on your skin, in your mouth, in the air, in the earth and in your food. They are so small that you need a microscope to see them.

Many kinds of bacteria are able to live inside you, but only a few of them make you sick. Most kinds are actually helpful. Some live in your intestines and graze on food that your body doesn't digest. At the same time, these bacteria make vitamins that your body needs.

The kinds of bacteria that make you sick produce substances called toxins. These toxins give you a fever, diarrhea, a headache, a bellyache, or other aches and pains. But sometimes it's your body's own germ-fighting methods that make you feel sick. That is because your white blood cells, which kill germs, also produce toxins.

Viruses are smaller than bacteria. Only a very powerful electron microscope can show you what they look like. Because they are so tiny, they can live inside your cells. In fact, a virus can't multiply unless it does get into a cell. When that happens, the virus actually forces your cell to stop its own activities and begin creating new viruses instead. Your cell may produce hundreds of exact copies of the original virus before it bursts open and dies. Then the newly made viruses find other cells to invade. They keep on multiplying until your body can produce enough antibodies to stop them. Meanwhile dead cells, plus broken pieces of germ-fighting white blood cells, make you sick.

Because they kill cells when they multiply, all viruses are harmful. Most people get some kind of viral illness once in a while. But the body usually fights it off quickly and the person is soon well again.

Why Do You Get a Stomachache?

Eating too much or too fast can give you a stomachache. Feeling worried or unhappy can, too. And sometimes your stomach hurts because you eat food in which certain bacteria have been growing. Poisons produced by these bacteria can give you a stomachache—but mainly they make you want to vomit.

Vomiting is so important to your body's safety that there is a special center for it in your brain. As soon as this center receives the signal that your stomach must get rid of something, messages go out over several nerves.

Muscles in your abdomen tighten up.

You hold your breath. This keeps vomit from getting into your lungs.

Your diaphragm, together with the muscles in your abdomen, squeezes hard against your stomach. And up comes the stuff that is making you sick. Once that happens, you feel much better.

What Makes a
Sore Throat Hurt?

Bacteria give you a sore throat. As they multiply in the throat's moist lining, they produce chemicals that make your body's cleanup team spring into action.

First the capillaries—the tiny blood vessels under the surface of your throat—expand. More blood pours through them, and your throat gets hot and red.

By now, white blood cells, your body's germ fighters, have started rushing to the spot. Under a microscope a white cell looks like a soft blob. It moves by stretching itself out and forming a sort of foot. The foot pokes its way through the thin capillary wall, and then the whole white cell slithers out in pursuit of germs.

To catch a germ, the white cell simply reaches out, surrounds the invader, then digests it. Soon the white cells produce irritating chemicals of their own. These can damage other cells, but they are a necessary part of the clean-up operation.

While this is going on, liquid seeps out of the blood into the throat's lining. This makes it swell. Pain signals, caused by the swelling and the damaged cells, travel along nerves with a message to your brain: sore throat!

Most sore throats don't last long. But if your doctor says you have something called strep throat, you'll probably be given medicine to cure it.

Why Does Poison Ivy Make You Itch?

The leaves of the poison ivy plant contain an oily chemical that makes most people miserable if they touch it. In a few hours the skin gets red and itchy. Later, blisters form. This happens to four out of every five people. Doctors say these people are allergic to poison ivy.

The oily stuff in the plant's leaves cause certain cells in your body to make chemicals

called antibodies. First, the antibodies hook up with the molecules of poison ivy oil. Then those two linked molecules make certain cells release another strong chemical called histamine. Histamine makes your skin get red, swollen and itchy.

Other allergies work the same way. People with hay fever make antibodies to pollen from flowers. If they breathe in the pollen, histamine is released. They sneeze and get runny noses and red itchy eyes.

All sorts of different things can cause allergies—eggs, milk, wheat, dust, cat dandruff, even medicines. It's easy to see why the body makes antibodies that fight disease germs. But why fight food and other things that seem harmless? And why do some people have allergies while others don't? The reason for allergies is still a puzzle.

What Good Is a Fever?

A fever makes you feel uncomfortably hot. But most doctors think a slight temperature isn't bad. If it goes up from 98.6 degrees Fahrenheit to 102 or 103, it isn't dangerous. And it may actually help your body to fight germs that cause the fever.

When disease germs multiply in your body, they produce poisonous chemicals called toxins. Your blood carries the toxins around to your brain, and there they affect a cluster of cells that control your temperature. Acting like a thermostat, the cells send out signals for your body to heat up.

Sometimes you shiver when you are getting a fever. This makes your body warmer, because your muscle cells are working and burning more food. Your blood heats up. Your heart beats faster. Even your sense of

time speeds up! You may think it's noon when it's really just the middle of the morning.

The extra heat may keep some kinds of germ from multiplying. That's the good part of a fever. But if your temperature rises too much, the fever can harm some of your cells, and the doctor will probably give you medicine to cool you down.

When the toxin-making germs have been killed, the thermostat in the brain turns down the heat, and your temperature becomes normal again.

What Do Drugs Do?

There are good drugs and bad drugs. The good ones are the ones the doctor gives you when you really need them. The bad drugs are the ones that somebody may ask you to try just for fun. If you ask, "Why should I?" you'll get this kind of answer: "It makes you feel great! *Everybody* is doing it. No, it can't do you any harm."

Some people do find drugs exciting—at first. But then comes the hard news: No matter what kind of drug it is, it can be

dangerous. Sooner or later your body will begin to tell you that it's not your body any more. It belongs to the drug, which now doesn't make you feel great. When you don't have the drug, you feel you must get it some way—any way. And you're scared of what it has done to you. But by that time you have the habit.

Smoking is a habit, too, and tobacco is a drug. People who smoke are more likely to get lung cancer than nonsmokers. They are also more likely to die of other diseases. Scientists' reports on thousands of people show that smokers and drug users get sick more often and die sooner than those who never got the habit. Why take a chance?

If you're curious, try this: Ask your gym teacher or school counselor for a good book that tells the real truth about what drugs do to you.

Chapter 5
YOU AND YOUR
WONDERFUL BRAIN

How Does Your Brain Think?

The biggest and most important part of your brain is the cerebrum. It is wrinkled and gray on the outside and white inside. A groove runs through it, separating the right half from the left.

The cerebrum is the only part of your brain that thinks. Some nerves connected with it bring messages from your eyes, ears, skin and muscles. Other nerves send messages out to them. These nerves are bundles of fine fibers. Inside your brain, the fibers are connected with microscopic nerve cells. These cells connect with one another and pass along bits of information.

Billions of tiny nerve cells are crowded into your cerebrum. Each has a cell body with one long fiber and hundreds of branching fibers. When nerve-to-nerve connections are made, the fiber branches act as switches. There are so many branches that your brain can make trillions of different connections. It can combine information in an almost endless number of ways. That's why you have such complicated thoughts, and why you know so much.

How Big Is Your Brain?

When you were born, you couldn't say a word, and you didn't know a thing, but your brain was all set to start learning. The fifty billion nerve cells now in your cerebrum were already in place. Not a single new one has been added since.

Yet your brain has grown. When you were born it weighed about a pound. By the time you were walking, your head and brain had doubled in size. And by the time you started first grade, your head and brain were about the size they are now.

If no new nerve cells were added to your brain, how did it get bigger? The nerve cells—

neurons—were not the only cells in it. There were lots of sticky cells, too. Scientists call them glia, which simply means glue cells. These glue cells grew. When they reached a certain size, they split in half, and new ones formed. Now there are more glue cells than neurons in your brain.

The neurons have never split, but they did grow. Their fibers became longer, and each day more branches sprouted from them.

Now each neuron has so many branches that it can connect with one of its neighbors in over a thousand different ways. Some neurons can make sixty thousand different connections.

What Does Your Brain Do Besides Think?

A section in the middle of your brain never thinks. It feels. It receives messages from inside your body, while the thinking part of your brain is busy with messages from the outside.

This thoughtless section—the between brain—has several divisions. One group of its cells sends pain signals to the thinking part of your brain when you get hurt. Another group sends out signals that cause feelings of pleasure. A nearby cluster of cells works as an alarm system. Some cells in this cluster send out warning messages that make you feel afraid, and other cells in the cluster throw you into a rage.

A tiny bulb the size of a pea hangs beneath this section. It is called the pituitary gland. Chemicals from the gland go directly into your blood and then all over your body. These chemicals make your bones grow, and they also trigger other glands.

The pituitary is prodded into action by its prune-sized neighbor which is sometimes called the "dumb brain." Its real name is the hypothalamus. All day and all night it receives messages from your inside organs, and it sends out messages to them. It lets you know when you are hungry and thirsty, and it makes sure your body stays at just the right temperature.

Two fist-sized knobs in the back of your brain form the cerebellum, and they control your balance and your aim. When you play softball, the cerebellum makes sure your hands swing the bat and that your feet carry you to first base when you make a hit.

In front of the cerebellum is the brainstem where a network of nerves keeps you alert. Although it is thoughtless, it helps the thinking part of your brain to do its best work.

What Happens to People When They "Black Out"?

The brain is an electric powerhouse, and its cells constantly produce current. To keep working they must have food and oxygen. The blood brings them these supplies. Every minute, the heart pumps about three cups of blood into two big blood vessels at the sides of the neck and then through narrow vessels that go all through the brain. One fifth of the oxygen your body needs is used by the brain!

If an accident slows down or shuts off the flow of blood, the brain cells may not get enough oxygen. This causes a blackout—sudden unconsciousness. A blackout may also happen when someone—a soldier on guard duty, for example—has to stand still for hours. Blood collects in his legs, not enough gets to his brain, and he blacks out, or faints. An illness, too, can upset the blood supply to the brain. So can the shock of bad news.

When people black out, they often fall. This may do some good by lowering the head, making it easier for the heart to pump blood to the brain.

Where Do Ideas Come From?

You really can say you have two brains, just as you have two eyes and ears, two arms and legs. The groove in the cerebrum, the top part of your brain, divides it into two halves. Each half has a separate set of nerves that connect it with one side of your body.

The connections are not the ones you would expect. The left half of the brain controls the right side of the body; the right half controls the left side.

The left and right sides of the brain are

different in some special ways. In many people the left side contains a group of nerves called the speech center. So that side usually handles most problems that deal with words. It brings together memories of words and of numbers. Then it uses them to figure out answers to questions. This side of the brain is where scientific ideas are likely to start.

The right side of the brain, in these people, has a different set of nerve connections. They are used when a person recognizes a famous movie star, learns to play the guitar, and figures out where objects are placed in the space around them. This side of the brain is the artistic side. When people draw or play an instrument, their ideas about art and music are likely to start in the right brain.

The right and left brains are connected by a bridge of nerves. This makes it possible for them to think together. Sing a song, and your two brains work as a team. While your left brain handles the words, your right brain handles the tune.

Scientists are finding that this division of work is not exactly the same in all people. Some have speech centers in the right brain, for example. Why is this so? That is still a mystery.

What's an IQ Test?

I is for intelligence and Q is for quotient. An IQ is written in numbers, and an IQ test is supposed to measure thinking ability.

Note that word "supposed."

At one time teachers and psychologists believed that intelligence, like blue eyes or big ears, was a trait you were born with. They were sure it could be measured.

Psychologists designed tests that seemed very scientific at first. The tests were supposed to measure how much thinking ability children had. But they actually measured how much children had learned.

After a while people began to wonder about the results of the tests. Why did city children seem to have higher IQ's than country children? It turned out that many of the test questions were about life in the city. Country children had not learned about city life, and so they often gave wrong answers.

Black children and Indian children had the same problem. The tests asked about things that came up in the lives of white children, but were often unfamiliar to black and Indian children.

What about children who did well on an

arithmetic test but poorly on the word questions? Were they half-smart and half-dumb?

Finally, it became clear that intelligence is not like big ears. There is no single trait that can be called intelligence. But there are many ways of being smart. That is why many schools no longer give IQ tests. Instead, children are given many different tests to find their strong and weak points. Then they can be helped to get over their weak points and to develop their strong ones.

How Does Your Memory Work?

What goes on in your brain when it learns and then remembers what it learned? That is still a great puzzle. Some scientists think that when information comes along a nerve pathway in the brain, the nerve itself changes. Perhaps these pathways are rather like a road map. Somehow your brain can search through them and find the right map when you want to remember something.

Other scientists think that information is stored at the gap between two nerve cells in the brain. Chemicals in this gap help electric current to pass from one cell to another, and perhaps these chemical links are somehow made stronger as you learn.

Does your brain store away a record of everything in your life? What happens to all the information that your eyes and other sense organs pick up? Are millions of places and faces and feelings hidden somewhere, even though you can't recall them? Perhaps there is room enough in your brain's fifty billion nerve cells to hold it all. Some scien-

tists think so. Others say that the brain keeps only certain information that seems important. But do you have an importance detector? What makes it work? Scientists still do not know. But they expect that by using brain power they will solve some of the brain's mysteries.

What Is Your Mind and Where Is It?

You were born with a brain, but not with a mind! You, yourself, created your mind. You developed it by using your brain, and by remembering things you have felt and seen and heard. Naturally, you do not remember everything. You almost always forget a phone number that you haven't used for awhile. Yet you remember people's faces, places you have seen, songs, tastes, smells, colors, ideas. These long-lasting memories form your mind.

You already have millions of memories and will have millions more. Your brain stops growing, but your mind does not. It will grow as long as you live.

What Is a Genius?

According to a saying by Thomas Edison, genius is 1 percent inspiration and 99 percent perspiration. Many special abilities—talents—go into the making of a great scientist or musician. But in addition to having talents, a genius must work hard and develop skills.

Some geniuses show their abilities when they are children. Mozart began to compose beautiful music at the age of five. Isaac Newton, who discovered the law of gravity, could solve college math problems when his classmates were still learning to add. But signs of genius rarely appear at an early age.

Some people are especially talented because they think creatively. That is, they put old ideas together to form completely new ideas. Can people be taught to think more creatively? No one knows. But asking the question is the first step in finding the answer.